I love rea

Animal Hospital

by Leonie Bennett

Editorial consultant: Mitch Cronick

Copyright © **ticktock Entertainment Ltd 2006**
First published in Great Britain in 2006 by **ticktock Media Ltd.,**
Unit 2, Orchard Business Centre, North Farm Road, Tunbridge Wells, Kent TN2 3XF

We would like to thank: Shirley Bickler and Suzanne Baker

ISBN 1 86007 998 9 pbk
Printed in China

Picture credits
t=top, b=bottom, c=centre, l-left, r=right, OFC= outside front cover
Corbis: 11, 12-13. Superstock: 4, 5, 6, 15, 16, 17, 19, 20, 21.

CONTENTS

Words that look **bold like this** are in the glossary.

I'm a vet

My name's Sam and I'm a vet.

I work in an animal hospital.

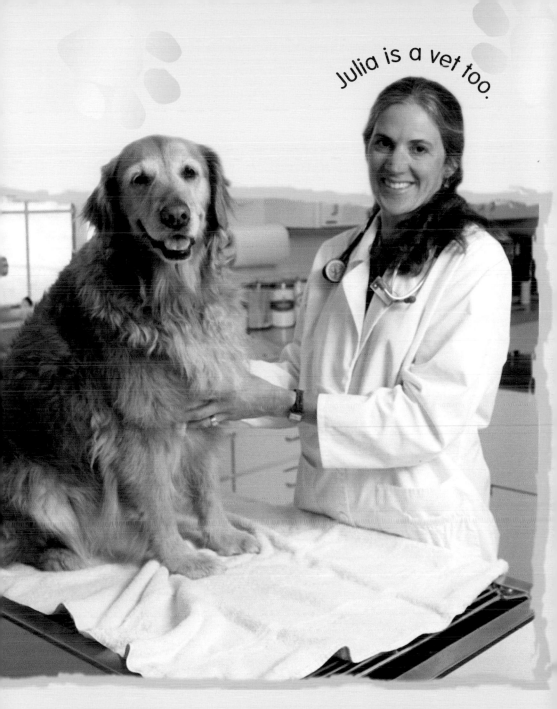

Julia is a vet too.

It takes five years to train to be a vet.

We need to know how to look after all sorts of animals.

5

The animals we see

Here are some of the animals that we take care of.

Small dogs

Big dogs

Guinea pigs

Rabbits

Parrots

Sometimes people find lost animals and bring them to the hospital.

This cat was found in a shed.

He was very tired and hungry.

Rescue cat

We checked him all over and gave him food and water.

Then he was taken to a **rescue centre**.

The helpers at the centre will try to find his owners.

The things we use

Here are some of the things we use in our work.

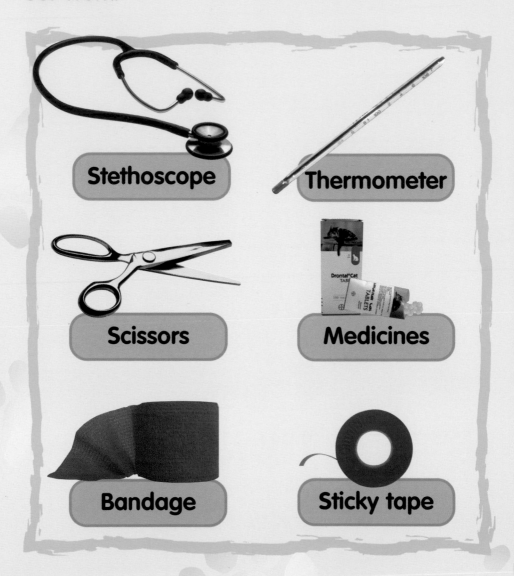

Stethoscope

Thermometer

Scissors

Medicines

Bandage

Sticky tape

We use x-rays to look inside animals.
An x-ray is a special photograph.

X-ray

This x-ray shows the bones in a
cat's tail and legs.

Syringe

We use a **syringe** to give **injections**.

Why do animals come to the hospital?

This dog fell off a wall and hurt her paw.

We will take an x-ray to see if any bones are broken.

This dog has a cut on his leg. We will make sure there is no **infection** and put a clean bandage on it.

Flea powder

Flea & Tick
Powder
for Dogs & Cats

Controls Flea & Tick

For Use on Dogs & Cats
12 Weeks of Age or Older

KEEP OUT
OF REACH OF CHILDREN
CAUTION

NET WEIGHT: 5 OZ (142 g)

This cat scratches herself a lot because she has **fleas.**

We will put some powder on her fur that will kill the fleas but will not hurt the cat.

Injections

Many pets come to the animal hospital to have injections to stop them from getting ill.

Cats are injected against cat flu and dogs are injected against kennel cough.

Syringe

This kitten is seven weeks old and is having her first injection.

She looks scared, but it won't hurt.

Alfie's story

Alfie is a friendly dog who scratches his head a lot.

I always check every animal all over, so I feel Alfie's tummy and listen to his heart with a **stethoscope.**

Everything inside Alfie is fine.

Nurse

Stethoscope

Alfie's bad ear

I look in Alfie's eyes and in his mouth.

When I check Alfie's ears, I find the problem.

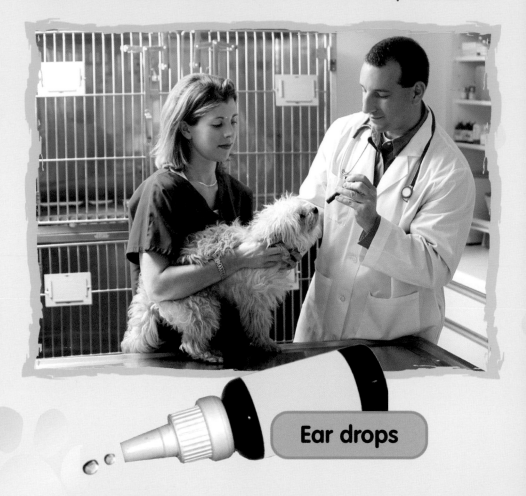

Ear drops

He has an ear infection so I put some drops in his ear which will make it better.

I put a large plastic collar around Alfie's neck so that he can't scratch his ear.

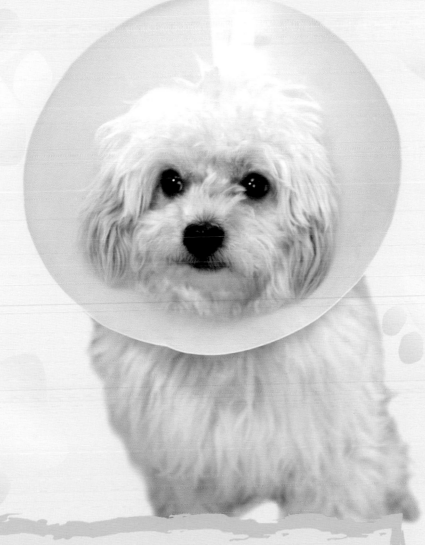

Now Alfie can go home but he must come for another check-up next week.

Good boy, Alfie!

Suzie's check-up

Suzie is an old dog who has come for a regular check-up.

First, Julia listens to Suzie's heart and lungs.

Next, she takes her temperature with a **thermometer.**

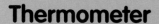

Thermometer

Julia uses a syringe to take some blood from Suzie.

Stethoscope

Later, Julia will test Suzie's blood to check that everything is normal.

19

Good girl, Suzie!

Julia checks Suzie's teeth. Then she puts her on the scales.

She sees that the dog weighs too much.

Julia tells Suzie's owner that he must not overfeed his dog or give her sweets and treats to eat.

Scales

If Suzie eats good food and goes for a walk every day she will keep fit.

Good girl, Suzie!

Thinking and talking about the animal hospital

What happened to this cat?

Why does this dog need to have an x-ray?

What pet would you like to have?

How would you look after it?

Why do you think vets have to train for five years?

What do you think would be the best and worst things about being a vet?

Glossary

fleas
Small insects which live on an animal or person's body.

infection
An illness caused by germs.

injection
Using a needle to put medicine inside an animal or a person.

rescue centre
A place where lost or unwanted animals are taken. Helpers take care of the animals and try to find them a place to live if they have no owners.

stethoscope
Instrument used to listen to an animal or person's heart and lungs.

syringe
A needle used to give injections.

thermometer
An instrument that tells us how warm or cold an animal or person is.

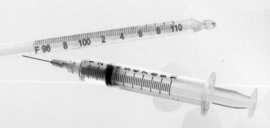